DOLPHINS

Heinemann
LIBRARY

Elizabeth Laskey

www.heinemann.co.uk
Visit our website to find out more information about Heinemann Library books.

To order:
☎ Phone 44 (0) 1865 888066
▤ Send a fax to 44 (0) 1865 314091
▧ Visit the Heinemann Bookshop at www.heinemann.co.uk to browse our catalogue and order online.

First published in Great Britain by Heinemann Library,
Halley Court, Jordan Hill, Oxford OX2 8EJ,
part of Harcourt Education Ltd.
Heinemann is a registered trademark of Harcourt
Education Ltd.

Edited by Barbara Katz, Kathy Peltan
Designed by Kimberly Saar, Heinemann Library
Illustrations and maps by John Fleck
Photo research by Bill Broyles
Production by John Nelson, Viv Hichins
Originated by Ambassador Litho Ltd.
Printed by Wing King Tong in Hong Kong

ISBN 0431 18204 3
07 06 05 04 03
10 9 8 7 6 5 4 3 2 1

British Library Cataloguing in Publication Data
Laskey, Elizabeth,
Dolphins. - (Sea creatures)
1.Dolphins - Juvenile literature
I.Title
599.5'3
A full catalogue record for this book is available from
the British Library.

Acknowledgments
The author and publishers are grateful to the
following for permission to reproduce copyright
material:
Cover photograph by Michael S. Nolan/Seapics.com

Title page, pp. 9, 14, 15T, 18, icons Doug
Perrine/Seapics.com; pp. 6, 8a Ingrid
Visser/Seapics.com; p. 5 James D. Watt/Watt
Wildlife Library/Visuals Unlimited; p. 7T François
Gohier/Ardea; pp. 7B, 8b Robert L.
Pitman/Seapics.com; p.10 J. Berghan/Seapics.com;
p. 11 James D. Watt/Seapics.com; pp. 13, 26 Ken
Lucas/Visuals Unlimited; pp. 15B, 29T Michael S.
Nolan/Seapics.com; p. 16 Brandon D. Cole; p. 17
Dr. Janet Mann/Georgetown University; p. 19 Jeffrey
Rotman/Photo Researchers, Inc.; pp. 20, 25 Flip
Nicklin/Minden Pictures; p. 21 Hulton Archive/Getty
Images; p. 22 Richard Frank Smith/Corbis Sygma;
p. 23 Thomas Jefferson/Seapics.com; p. 24 Paul
Kay/Oxford Scientific Films; p. 27 Sarasota Dolphin
Research Program/Mote Marine Laboratory; p. 28
Colin Monteath/Oxford Scientific Films; p. 29B
Dr. Ken Marten/Earthtrust

Special thanks to Dr Randall Wells and to Michael
Bright, Executive Producer, BBB Natural History Unit,
for their help in the preparation of this book.

Every effort has been made to contact copyright
holders of any material reproduced in this book. Any
omissions will be rectified in subsequent printings if
notice is given to the publishers.

Contents

You can find words in bold, **like this**, in the Glossary.

Where would you find a dolphin?

You are sitting in a boat off the coast of New Zealand (see map below), on a sunny March day. You look across the water and see eight grey triangle-shaped fins just above the surface. Your first thought is: sharks! But they are not sharks. The fins belong to some curious dusky dolphins. One of them decides to show off. It leaps out of the water and does a somersault in mid air. It is smooth and sleek, with a dark grey back and a white belly.

After a few minutes, the dolphins decide they have had enough of you. One leaps up, curves through the air and dives back in. Then the others all leap up and dive back in at exactly the same time. Soon they are out of sight.

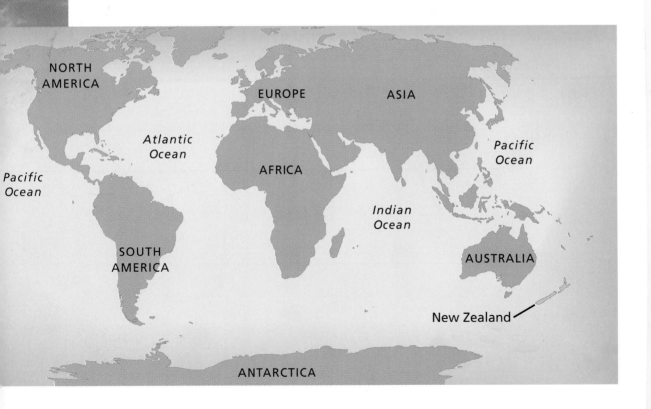

What kind of creature is a dolphin?

It is true that a dolphin looks a bit like a shark. But dolphins are not related to sharks, which are fish. Dolphins are a type of toothed whale. Like other whales, dolphins are **mammals**.

This baby Atlantic spotted dolphin drinks its mother's milk as she swims along.

A dolphin is a water mammal

Most **species** of dolphin live in the sea. But there are a few species, such as the boto dolphin, that live only in rivers. All mammals have certain things in common. They are all **warm-blooded.** This means that their body temperature always stays the same.

All mammals breathe air through lungs. Even though dolphins spend time underwater, they come to the surface to breathe air. Baby mammals drink milk made by their mothers' bodies. All mammals have some hair or fur. Dolphins are born with a few hairs on their **beak**, or jaw area, that disappear soon after birth.

How many kinds of dolphin are there?

There are 26 **species** we call dolphins living in the world's seas, and another five species living in rivers. Some species stay close to the coast. Others live far out at sea.

The bottlenose dolphin is the best known

Bottlenose dolphins are found in most parts of the world. Many live near coasts. They can be found off the coast of Scotland and as far south as Australia, Africa and South America. Bottlenose dolphins also live along the Atlantic and Pacific coasts of North America. Some bottlenose dolphins live in deeper waters. Bottlenose dolphins are grey and can range in size from 1.8 to 4 metres. The smaller ones are about the size of a tall man. The largest are taller than the height of a basketball hoop.

*Bottlenose dolphins have a long narrow **beak** that looks a bit like a bottle.*

Some species live close to coasts

The Atlantic white-sided dolphin is one species that spends most of its time close to the coast. These dolphins live in the colder waters of the Atlantic Ocean. They have black backs with white, grey and yellow streaks on their sides. They range in size from 1.8 to 2.4 metres. Hector's dolphins are small, plump grey dolphins that live near the New Zealand coast. They are about 1.2 to 1.5 metres long.

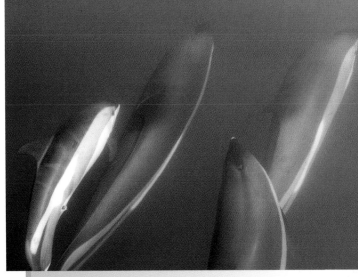

Atlantic white-sided dolphins often visit the west of Britain, mainly along the Scottish coast.

Other dolphins that live near the coast include the Indo-Pacific humpbacked dolphin and the Irrawaddy dolphin. These two species are unusual because they spend some time in rivers.

Extreme dolphins

These are hourglass dolphins, the one species that can live in icy waters. They are found near the South Pole. Even in summer the water temperature is only about 3°C, barely above freezing.

Some species live in deeper waters

Long-snouted spinner dolphins are most common in the deep, warm waters of the oceans. They are mainly grey, and range in size from about 1.2 to 2.1 metres. They are known for leaping into the air and spinning several times before dropping back into the water. Atlantic spotted dolphins and Pantropical spotted dolphins live in the warmest parts of the Atlantic and Pacific oceans. They have grey backs and white bellies. Their bodies have a sprinkling of dark or light spots.

The average length of a dusky dolphin is just over 1.8 metres.

Northern right whale dolphins do not have **dorsal fins**. They have black backs and white bellies that make them look rather like oversized penguins. They are 2 to 3 metres long. Other **species** found away from the coasts are the common dolphin, the striped dolphin and the rough-toothed dolphin.

Northern right whale dolphins have no dorsal fin on their backs.

How does a dolphin's body work?

Dolphins are excellent swimmers. Their bodies are very well adapted for life in the sea.

Striped dolphins have taller dorsal fins than most other dolphin species.

The tail moves a dolphin forwards

A dolphin's tail is made up of two triangle-shaped **tail flukes**. The tail flukes themselves do not have any muscles. Powerful muscles along the dolphin's **backbone** move the tail flukes up and down. This moves the dolphin forwards. The dolphin uses its **flippers** for steering and balance. Also, most dolphins have a dorsal fin on their back that helps them to steer and balance.

A layer of fatty **blubber** and smooth skin covers the bones and muscles and gives the dolphin its sleek shape. This shape helps the dolphin glide swiftly through the water.

A dolphin breathes through a hole on top of its head

The hole on top of a dolphin's head is called a **blowhole.** The blowhole leads to the dolphin's lungs. When a dolphin is underwater, a flap seals the blowhole shut and keeps water from getting into the dolphin's lungs. Just before the dolphin breaks the surface to breathe, it opens the blowhole to breathe out.

When a dolphin breathes out, a fountain of water called a **spout** sprays up into the air. The spout is a mixture of the air the dolphin has breathed out and water that was on the surface of the closed blowhole.

? Did you know?

A dolphin can breathe out and breathe in again in less than a fifth of a second.

Air leaves a dolphin's blowhole at more than 161 kilometres (100 miles) per hour, or more than three times the speed of a car on a town road.

The rough-toothed dolphin can hold its breath for fifteen minutes.

A dolphin can stay underwater for a long time

Dolphins do not take a big gulp of air and hold most of the air in their lungs when they go underwater. Dolphins do hold some air in their lungs, but they store most of the oxygen they need in their muscles and blood. Dolphins have at least twice as much blood as humans. This gives them more 'storage space' for oxygen. They use up this stored oxygen very slowly. These are some of the reasons why dolphins can stay underwater for a long time.

Most **species** can hold their breath for as long as seven minutes to make a deep dive. But dolphins usually stay underwater for only about two to three minutes. Most people can hold their breath only for about one minute.

A dolphin can see and hear very well

Dolphins have excellent eyesight. They see well both underwater and above water. Their eyes can roll so far sideways that they can almost see behind them. Dolphins hear much better than humans. They also have a special way of using sound called **echolocation**. To use echolocation, a dolphin makes clicking sounds. The clicks pass through a part of the dolphin's head called the **melon**, then move through the water (emitted sound). When the sounds hit an object, such as a fish or a rock, an 'echo' bounces back (reflected sound) to a fat-filled cavity in the dolphin's lower jaw. The way the echo sounds and how long it takes to get back to the dolphin tell the dolphin about the object's shape, what it is made of and how far away it is. Echolocation helps dolphins move around when it is too dark to see.

A dolphin can tell what kind of fish is near by just from listening to the echo.

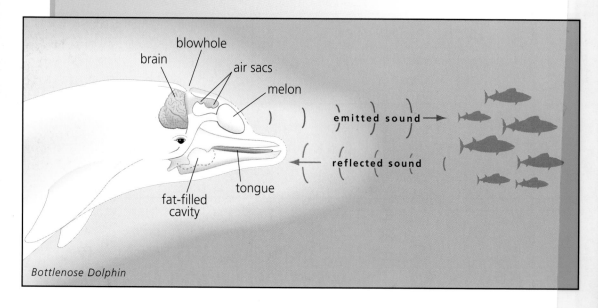

brain
blowhole
air sacs
melon
emitted sound →
reflected sound
tongue
fat-filled cavity

Bottlenose Dolphin

What do dolphins eat?

Dolphins eat different kinds of fish and other sea creatures. Dolphins eat a lot. A common dolphin eats up to 9 kilograms of fish each day. If you tried to eat that much food you would have to eat about 90 sandwiches!

Fish and squid are favourite foods

What a dolphin eats depends on what type of fish and other sea creatures live near by. For example, Commerson's dolphins living near the tip of South America eat sardines, anchovies, small shellfish and squid. Striped dolphins that live in the north Atlantic eat cod.

The northern right whale dolphin which lives in the deep waters of the northern Pacific, eats squid and a glow-in-the-dark type of fish called a lanternfish.

Dolphins have teeth, but they swallow their food whole, without chewing. They use their teeth to catch and hold food.

To catch a fish, a dolphin might use its **tail flukes** to slap the fish. Sometimes this makes the fish fly into the air. When the stunned fish lands back on the water surface, the dolphin catches it and eats it.

Dolphins sometimes work together to catch large numbers of fish. A group of six or more dolphins will form a circle around a large group of fish. As the dolphins circle, they close in on the fish to make the circle smaller. This pushes the fish into a tight group in the middle. Then the dolphins take turns darting into the circle to grab some fish. The other dolphins keep the fish trapped. A group of dolphins might also form a line behind a group of fish. Then they swim forward and push the fish towards another line of hungry dolphins.

These common dolphins are eating sardines off the coast of South Africa.

What do dolphins do?

Dolphins seem to like to have fun, jumping high out of the water and playing with other dolphins. They are very clever animals and are able to **communicate** with each other.

There are about 25 Atlantic spotted dolphins in this group. But a group may be as small as two or three dolphins.

Dolphins form groups

Dolphins form groups. Members of a group are usually not members of the same family. Scientists believe that one of the main reasons why dolphins form groups is for safety. It is much harder for a **predator** to attack a group of dolphins because it is hard for the predator to focus on a particular dolphin. Group members help each other. If one member is hurt, other group members may help the hurt dolphin to stay at the surface so it can breathe.

Dolphin predators

Orcas (killer whales) and large sharks eat dolphins, especially young dolphins. But some brave dolphins have been known to group together to chase away sharks that try to attack their group. Some dolphins, like the one shown here, have scars from shark attacks.

They jump and play

Dolphins are known for the high jumps and flips they can do. Spinner dolphins can twirl up to fourteen times in the air before diving back into the water. Dusky dolphins and some other **species** are known for **porpoising**, or leaping out and back into the water many times in a row. This helps them move very quickly and they do not get too tired. It is easier to move through air than through water.

Dolphins like to play. They chase each other and toss around clumps of seaweed. Scientists have also watched dolphins bump into pufferfish on purpose. They think that the dolphins do this for the fun of making the pufferfish puff up. But play has a purpose. It is one way for young dolphins to build strength and learn how to use their bodies. It can also help them to learn skills they will need later while hunting.

Striped dolphins have been seen doing backward somersaults and jumping as high as 7 metres. With such a leap, they could jump over the head of a giraffe.

16

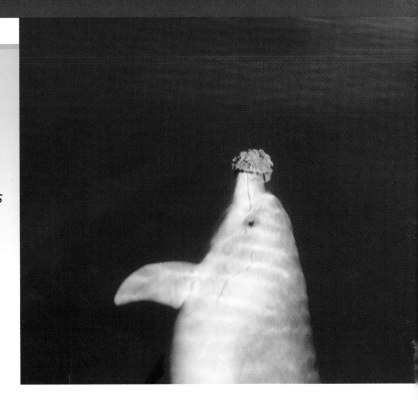

*This dolphin living in Shark Bay, Western Australia, is wearing a sponge on its **beak**. Some scientists think dolphins wear sponges to protect themselves while they look for food in rocky areas.*

They think and learn

Dolphins can learn and come up with new ideas. One female bottlenose dolphin worked out an easy way to catch fish. She put small pieces of fish in her open mouth and waited for a fish to come and take the bait. As soon as the fish entered her mouth, she clamped her jaws shut and swallowed the fish. A few days later other dolphins had learned her trick and were also catching fish this way.

Two clever dolphins

Two bottlenose dolphins outwitted an eel that had slithered into a narrow space. One dolphin picked up a spiky scorpion fish in its mouth. It poked the scorpion fish at the eel until the eel swam out of its hiding place. The dolphins were then able to catch it.

17

They communicate

Dolphins **communicate** with each other in several ways. For example, each dolphin has its own call, called a **signature whistle.** Other dolphins learn and remember the signature whistles of dolphins in their group. A mother dolphin will use her signature whistle if she and her baby have been separated and cannot see each other. The baby knows its mother's whistle and will call back with its own signature whistle. The mother can then find the baby.

Dolphins also make other **vocalizations** including squeaks, chirps and grunts. Squeaks may communicate that a dolphin is in trouble. Dolphins also use their bodies to communicate. Examples of this body language include shaking the head from side to side and rolling over and playing dead. Scientists are still working on finding out just what these signals mean.

Scientists think that when a dolphin opens and closes its mouth and blows bubbles it is showing anger.

What is dolphin family life like?

Many dolphin **species** form strong family and group bonds. The bond between a mother and her baby, or **calf**, is very strong.

The female gives birth

Female dolphins get pregnant about every two to four years. The pregnancy lasts about ten to twelve months. A calf is born tail first. As soon as the mother has given birth, she leads the calf to the surface for its first breath of air.

Newborn calves are not very big. A newborn long-snouted spinner dolphin is only about 71 to 86 centimetres long, or about as long as a tennis racket.

*A calf swims very close to its mother. This way the mother does most of the swimming work. The calf only has to pump its **tail flukes** from time to time. These are bottlenose dolphins.*

Dolphins can live for more than 40 years, but most dolphins do not live that long. Many die when they are still calves. The species shown here is the Atlantic spotted dolphin.

Young dolphins grow up slowly

For the first few months, calves depend completely on their mother's milk for food. Because both the mother and the calf have to go to the surface to breathe every few minutes, a **calf feeds** for a few seconds at a time.

After several months to a year, calves learn to hunt fish and other sea creatures. But they may still feed from their mother sometimes. Young bottlenose dolphins have been known to do this for four years or more.

After a few years, young dolphins go off on their own, or join a group of other young dolphins. A male bottlenose dolphin may pair up with another male, or join a group of males. A pregnant female dolphin may spend time with other pregnant dolphins. Females that already have calves may spend time with other dolphin mothers and their babies.

Are dolphins endangered?

The number of dolphins in the sea has fallen because of dolphin hunting and because of other human activities that can harm dolphins. Some dolphin **species** are **endangered**. This means that the species might die out, or become **extinct** in your lifetime or your children's lifetime.

Dolphins were hunted in the past

In the past, some dolphins were hunted for their meat. Also, many fishermen killed dolphins just to keep them from eating the fish they were trying to catch. One place where many dolphins were hunted was the Black Sea in Europe. Fishermen from countries that border the Black Sea, such as Russia and Turkey, began hunting dolphins in the late 1800s. In 1950, there were still about 1 million dolphins in the Black Sea. But by 1995, only 10,000 were left.

This dolphin was killed off the British coast near Bristol in the 1930s.

Some hunting still goes on

In some countries, dolphin hunting continues. In Japan, dolphin hunting is legal and more than 20,000 dolphins are killed each year. The meat is sold in supermarkets and served in restaurants. Some meat becomes pet food. In South America and the Caribbean, dolphin hunting goes on both legally and illegally. Dolphins are killed and eaten, or used as bait by people fishing for crabs.

Each year people in the Faroe Islands, near Iceland in the northern Atlantic Ocean, have a whale and dolphin hunt. They kill pilot whales, Atlantic white-sided dolphins and white-beaked dolphins.

In the past, eating the meat from these animals helped the people of the Faroe Islands make it through the winter. But today very little of the meat is eaten.

But many dolphins are now protected

Britain, the USA, Australia and many other countries have laws that protect dolphins from being harmed or killed. In Russia, dolphin hunting was outlawed in 1966, but it was still allowed in Turkey. Dolphins in the Black Sea were not fully protected until 2001.

Pollution harms dolphins

Chemicals from homes, farms and factories have washed into the sea. Many of these chemicals are poisonous. The poisons get into the bodies of fish that dolphins eat and so get into the dolphins' bodies. This can make the dolphins ill.

Only about 180 of these pink Indo-Pacific humpbacked dolphins are left in the polluted waters of the Pearl River Delta.

In 1987 and 1988, about 750 bottlenose dolphins washed up dead on beaches from New Jersey in the USA south along the Atlantic coast. Scientists found poisonous chemicals in their bodies. They also found **viruses** in their bodies. Scientists think the chemicals weakened the dolphins so that they could not fight the viruses.

Pollution is a big problem for a group of Indo-Pacific humpbacked dolphins known as the Pearl River Delta dolphins. This group lives between Hong Kong and China. The water is so polluted with sewage and chemicals that almost all the **calves** that are born die. This, of course, means that these dolphins could soon die out.

Dolphins die in fishing nets

In the last 40 years, about 7 million dolphins have died from being accidentally tangled in **purse seine nets** used to catch tuna. In some parts of the Pacific Ocean, large groups of tuna swim underneath dolphin groups. Purse seine boats follow the dolphins and then circle their net around the dolphins and the tuna. Dolphins get tangled in the net and drown because they cannot get to the surface to breathe.

Concerned people and **conservation** groups have spoken out against this needless killing of dolphins. In 1990, large tuna canning companies decided not to buy tuna that had been caught in a way that killed dolphins. Tuna caught in a 'dolphin safe' way is labelled to show that no dolphins were killed when the tuna was caught.

This harbour porpoise was killed by ghost fishing. This means the net was lost or thrown away by the fishermen. Dolphins can also die this way.

How do we learn about dolphins?

When scientists first began studying dolphins, they studied captive dolphins. They learned a lot about how dolphins' bodies worked, their behaviour and how they use sound. Scientists still study dolphins in captivity. However, a dolphin's natural habitat is a better place to learn how it finds food, avoids **predators** and finds a mate.

This scientist is putting an underwater microphone to the dolphin so that he can listen to the whistles it makes.

Dolphins in captivity

In the USA, dolphins have been kept in sea parks since the 1930s. For many years, all the dolphins were captured in the wild. Since the 1980s, captive breeding programmes have supplied most of the dolphins on display. However, some **aquariums** still capture wild dolphins. In the USA, South Carolina is the only state that has banned dolphin shows. In Britain, it is illegal to keep a dolphin in captivity at a sea park or aquarium.

Scientists have learned a lot from captive dolphins. But some people want to see dolphin shows stopped.

Trainers teach dolphins to show behaviours on command and not just when they want to. This helps sea park visitors learn about dolphins. They also train the dolphins to allow a **vet** to touch them so they can have their health checked. In the USA, the government has rules about how dolphins should be cared for. But some dolphins in other countries do not have clean water, big tanks and proper food.

Scientists collect data on wild dolphins

Since 1970, scientists have been studying a group of bottlenose dolphins living off the coast of Sarasota, Florida in the USA. They have collected **data** on more than 2500 dolphins. Some of the young dolphins they are now studying are the great-grandchildren of the first dolphins studied. They now know details of their lives, such as where the dolphins go to find food and how often **calves** are born.

Scientists study how human activities affect dolphins

Human activities may change dolphins' normal activity patterns. For example, there are many more boats in the waters off Sarasota than there used to be. Scientists already knew that dolphins had been hurt and sometimes killed when boats hit them. They also wanted to know how boats and boat noise affect the dolphins' behaviour. Scientists learned that when boats came near dolphins, the dolphins dived deeper, swam faster and stayed underwater longer than they would have if no boats were near. If they have to avoid boats every day and do it lots of times every day, it is bad for their health.

Information like this helps lawmakers decide on laws to protect dolphins. Knowing that boats bother dolphins might lead to a rule that would keep boats away from certain areas. Protecting dolphins will make sure that these wonderful sea creatures continue to be part of the world's **biodiversity**.

Scientists in Florida, USA use a video camera attached to an airship to record how dolphins act underwater when boats are near by.

✔ The northern right whale dolphin can leap across a distance of 7 metres, which would be like jumping across four cars parked next to each other.

✔ The chubby Commerson's dolphin usually takes two or three quick breaths before diving. This may be how it got the nickname 'puffing pig'. Because of its black and white colouring, it is also sometimes called the skunk dolphin.

The Commerson's dolphin has a rounded dorsal fin.

✔ In Vietnam, the Irrawaddy dolphin is sacred, or very special. If a dead Irrawaddy dolphin is found, it will be given a funeral.

✔ Bottlenose dolphins off South Carolina in the USA have been known to chase fish out of the water and on to the beach.

✔ Bottlenose dolphins can dive as deep as 500 metres. That's ten times as long as an Olympic swimming pool.

✔ Some long-snouted spinner dolphins have as many as 252 teeth, more than any other **species** of dolphin.

☑ Spinner dolphins and other dolphins living in warm waters have to watch out for a small shark known as the cookie-cutter shark. This shark attaches its mouth to a dolphin's body and takes a cookie-shaped bite out of the dolphin's flesh.

☑ Older Risso's dolphins are sometimes so scratched and scarred that their grey bodies look almost white. This is because other Risso's dolphins scrape them with their teeth and the scratches turn into white scars.

☑ Dolphins and porpoises are both water **mammals**, but there are differences. Porpoises are usually smaller, and they have fatter bodies than most dolphins. Most of the six species of porpoise have a small **dorsal fin** shaped like a triangle, but do not have a **beak.** A dolphin's dorsal fin is shaped like a sickle. It looks like a sliver of the moon.

Risso's dolphins can have up to fourteen teeth in their lower jaw. They have no teeth in their upper jaw.

Captive and wild bottlenose dolphins have been spotted blowing bubble rings and playing with them.

Glossary

aquarium building where people can see sea creatures that are on display. It is also a single tank that holds fish or other water animals.

backbone bone that stretches down the middle of the back

beak jaw area that may be somewhat pointed towards the front

biodiversity all the different kinds of plants and animals on Earth

blowhole hole in a dolphin's head that leads to the lungs and is used for breathing

blubber a layer of fat under a dolphin's skin

calf (plural is **calves**) baby dolphin

conservation the protection of the natural world

communicate share information

data facts and information

dorsal fin triangle-shaped body part on the back of most species of dolphin

driftnet large fishing net that may stretch for miles

echolocation a way dolphins use sound and echoes to help them find their way

endangered in danger of dying out

extinct when a species has completely died out

flipper wing-shaped body part that dolphins use to help them balance and steer while they swim. It has bones in it.

habitat place where an animal lives in the wild

mammal member of a group of animals that are warm-blooded, have hair or fur and drink milk made by their mothers

melon rounded mass of fat inside the front of a dolphin's head

porpoising leaping out and back into the water while moving forwards

predator animal that attacks and kills another type of animal

purse seine net fishing net used to catch tuna. The net is circled around a group of fish and then a drawstring on the bottom is pulled to close the net around the fish.

signature whistle whistle call that dolphins use to identify themselves. Each dolphin has a signature whistle that is different from that of others.

species group of animals that have the same features and can have babies with each other

spout spray of water and air that rises above the surface of the sea when a dolphin breathes out and is about to come to the surface

tail flukes a dolphin's tail

vet animal doctor

virus microscopic organism that can get into an animal's body and make it ill

vocalizations squeaks, chirps, grunts, whistles and other sounds made by dolphins

warm-blooded being able to keep the body temperature the same at all times

More books to read

Dolphins. Michael Bright (BBC Worldwide, 2001)

Really Wild: Dolphins. Claire Robinson (Heinemann Library, 2000)

Whales, Dolphins and Porpoises. Mark Cawardine. (Dorling Kindersley, 2000)

Natural World: Dolphins. Nic Davies (Hodder Wayland, 2000)

Index

Titles in the *Sea Creatures* series include:

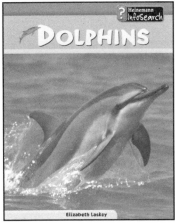

Hardback   0 431 18204 3

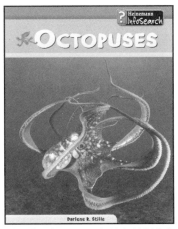

Hardback   0 431 18200 0

Hardback   0 431 18201 9

Hardback   0 431 18205 1

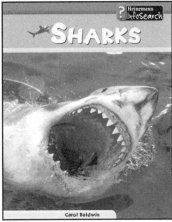

Hardback   0 431 18203 5

Hardback   0 431 18202 7

Find out about the other titles in this series on our website www.heinemann.co.uk/library